SO-AWI-327

Mission to MARS!

by Paul Beck

Welcome to the lab!
To assemble and launch your rocket right away, turn to page 28!

Mission to Mars!

© 2007 becker&mayer! LLC, 11120 NE 33rd Place, Suite 101, Bellevue, Washington.

Published by SmartLab®, an imprint of becker&mayer!
All rights reserved. SmartLab® is a registered trademark of becker&mayer!,
11120 NE 33rd Place, Suite 101, Bellevue, Washington.
Creative development by Jim Becker, Anna Johnson, and Aaron Tibbs

No part of this book may be reproduced, stored in a retrieval system, or transmitted in any form
or by any means, electronic, mechanical, photocopying, recording, or otherwise, without the prior
permission of SmartLab®. Requests for such permissions should be addressed to SmartLab® Permissions,
becker&mayer!, 11120 NE 33rd Place, Suite 101, Bellevue, Washington 98004.

If you have questions or comments about this product,
please visit www.smartlabtoys.com/customerservice.html
and click on Customer Service Request Form.

Edited by Ben Grossblatt
Written by Paul Beck
Art Direction by Eddee Helms
Package illustration by Jeremy Friesen
Package design by Wade Sherrard
Book interiors designed by Tyler Freidenrich, Brandon Walker, and Scott Westgard
Illustrations by Tyler Freidenrich, Ryan Hobson, and Gabe Stromberg
Assembly and launch illustrations by Ryan Hobson
SmartLab® character photography by Craig Harrold
Product development by Breanna Guidotti
Production management by Blake Mitchum and Beth Lenz
Project management by Beth Lenz
Additional image research by Zena Chew

Image credits:

Pages 3, 5, 13: Mars image from NASA/JPL-Caltech; Page 4: Images of Mars, Phobos, and Deimos
from NASA/JPL-Caltech; Page 5: Valles Marineris image from NASA's Viking Project; Pages 6, 7:
Artist's renderings of the Ares launch vehicles, crew exploration vehicle, and lunar lander from NASA's
Constellation Program; Pages 7, 26: Mars concept illustrations produced for NASA by John Frassanito
and Associates. Technical concepts from NASA's Planetary Projects Office, Johnson Space Center; Page
9: Artist's rendering of the Orion spacecraft docked at the International Space Station (ISS) for NASA's
Constellation Program; Page 9, 12: Mars image courtesy of NASA, ESA, The Hubble Heritage Team
(STScI/AURA), J. Bell (Cornell University), and M. Wolff (Space Science Institute); Page 13: Titan aeroshell
entry illustration from NASA's Solar System Exploration multimedia gallery; Pages 18, 19, 21, 25: Images
of astronaut Sunita L. Williams, cosmonaut Vladimir N. Dezhurov, cosmonaut Fyodor N. Yurchikhin, and
European Space Agency astronaut Thomas Reiter on the International Space Station, from NASA's Human
Space Flight photo gallery; Page 23: Space suit image from NASA's Glenn Research Center.

Every effort has been made to correctly attribute all the material reproduced in this book.
We will be happy to correct any errors in future editions.

Printed, manufactured, and assembled in China, May 2010 by Winner Printing & Packaging Ltd.

Mission to Mars! is part of the SmartLab® *Remote Control Rocket* kit. Not to be sold separately.

4 5 6 7 13 12 11 10

Distributed in the UK & ROI by:
Brainstorm, Ltd., Mill Lane, Gisburn
Lancashire BB7 4LN UK

ISBN-13: 978-1-932855-99-9
ISBN-10: 1-932855-99-8
10889

MISSION TO MARS

You're about to leave Earth for the grandest adventure of all: a trip to Mars. It will take you seven months to get there, and after only a brief stay, it will take you 10 months to get back. The whole trip, the shortest one possible for visiting the Red Planet, will take you a year and a half.

The planets are only aligned correctly for a trip to Mars once every 26 months. If you miss your window of opportunity, it's going to be more than two years before you get another chance.

You and the rest of the crew will be completely on your own. If anything goes wrong, a rescue mission would have to wait for the next available launch window.

Your Mars mission handbook is packed with information: science, tricks, and knowledge no astronaut can live without.

YOUR JOB

You're going to Mars partly just to show that it can be done, and partly to work out the kinks for longer missions in the future. You'll check out the natural resources to see how they can be used by the explorers who will follow in your footsteps. And you'll make excursions on the planet to look for signs of past or present life. You are not just an astronaut—you are an ambassador from planet Earth!

QUICK FACTS

Mars is the fourth planet in the solar system, named for the Roman god of war. Its nickname, the Red Planet, comes from its color, noticeable even when viewed from Earth with the naked eye.

DIAMETER:

4,222 miles, just a bit more than half the diameter of Earth.

LENGTH OF MARTIAN DAY:

24 hours, 37 minutes – slightly longer than one Earth day.

LENGTH OF MARTIAN YEAR:

1.88 Earth years, or 687 Earth days (that's 669 Mars days).

MOONS:

Two, Phobos and Deimos. Both are tiny. Phobos is only 13 miles in diameter, and Deimos is a mere 8 miles.

TEMPERATURE:

Ranges from -225°F to 80°F, depending on season, location, and distance above the ground. Because of the thin atmosphere, even if the temperature at the soles of your feet is a balmy 80°, the temperature at your head will be below freezing.

Phobos

Deimos

Astronomers measure the distances to planets in astronomical units, or AU for short. One AU is very close to the average distance from Earth to the sun, or 93 million miles. Mars's average distance is 1.52 AU.

MAJOR ATTRACTIONS

Look for these spectacular features while you're orbiting the planet.

VALLES MARINERIS

The Valles Marineris, or Mariner Valleys, are a system of canyons as long as the United States is wide. This grandest canyon of the solar system is more than 6 miles deep at its deepest point. That's six times the depth of the Grand Canyon on Earth.

OLYMPUS MONS

Mars also features the biggest volcano in the solar system, Olympus Mons. This shield volcano is more than 16 miles high, but its 300-mile diameter gives it a gentle slope. Olympus Mons has a four-mile-high ring of cliffs around its perimeter.

POLAR ICE CAPS

Mars has ice caps at its northern and southern poles. It's carbon dioxide ice, like the "dry ice" you're familiar with on Earth. There is also water ice under both ice caps.

SPACE SHIPS

It's going to take four different, specialized spacecraft to get you to Mars and back. Here's an overview.

HEAVY-LIFT LAUNCH VEHICLE

CREW TRANSFER VEHICLE (THE TAXI)
Your shuttlecraft to and from the surface of the earth.

CREW LAUNCH VEHICLE

HIGH ORBIT VEHICLE (THE TUG)
The job of this robotic ship is to tow the Mars/Earth Transfer Vechicle to high Earth orbit.

To astronauts, a launch vehicle is a rocket that carries a payload. It's the push that gets you and your ships into space. Non-astronauts call these "rockets."

MARS LANDER AND ASCENT VEHICLE (THE MINIVAN)

This is your landing craft, home on Mars, and transportation back up to the Transfer Vehicle in Mars orbit. This craft will make its trip from Earth to Mars robotically, without a crew on board. You'll move into it once you reach Mars orbit.

Mars ascent stage: Small shuttlecraft for returning you from the surface to Mars orbit

Mars surface habitat: Your home away from home, where you'll live while exploring the Red Planet. Part of the habitat is a super-strong inflatable structure.

Lander stage: For landing on the surface

MARS/EARTH TRANSFER VEHICLE (THE BUS)

Its job is to get you to Mars, then wait in orbit to take you back to Earth. It consists of the Mars Transfer Habitat (more on that later), a rocket engine stage for getting you from Earth to Mars, another one for getting you back, and an aeroshell for using the thin upper atmospheres of both planets for putting you in orbit.

TIME LINE

Your trip to Mars will last only one and a half years, so you'll want to savor every moment!

BEFORE YOU BLAST OFF

T -9 MONTHS: The tug will carry the components of the Mars ship (the bus) into orbit.

T -1 WEEK: The bus will await your arrival, traveling in a long, elliptical orbit. It will swing from perigee (closest to Earth) of about 200 miles, to apogee (farthest from Earth) of 500 miles.

T 0: BLAST OFF

You and your crewmates will leave Earth aboard the taxi. The trip from Earth to space will take about eight minutes.

T +1 HOUR: SECOND SHIP

The crew transport capsule will dock with the bus. You will cross over, and the space taxi will head back to Earth.

T +2 DAYS: TO MARS

The ship's computers will fire the engine of the trans-Mars rocket stage. The rocket burn will push you out of orbit and on your path to Mars.

TAXI

BUS

TO MARS

BACK TO EARTH

T +1.5 YEARS: TOUCHDOWN

As your ship nears Earth, the aerocapture system will slow your speed to place the ship in low-Earth orbit.

The space taxi will be waiting for you. After rendezvous and docking, you and your crewmates will cross to the capsule for your Earthside return. You will touch down on your home planet a year and a half after your departure. Please remain seated until the capsule has come to a complete stop.

No one says "one week before blast-off." The pros use T to mean the Big Moment. So T -9 months means 9 months before liftoff.

Docked: Orion spacecraft docked at the International Space Station.

T +7 MONTHS: THE RED PLANET

The long cruise ends when your ship's aerocapture system slows it down to orbital speed around Mars.

While you have been traveling, the crewless minivan will have made the same journey to a spot in Mars orbit nearby. You will rendezvous, dock, and board the surface module. Using first aerobraking and then parachutes, you will descend in the lander to touch down on the Martian surface.

The real work begins! You and your crewmates will spend a month conducting research and continuing previous crews' tests for a future long-term Mars base.

MINIVAN →

Astronauts never say "meet up with." It's always rendezvous (RON-day-voo).

T +8 MONTHS: HOMEWARD BOUND

You will leave the surface and climb back into space aboard the Mars ascent module, leaving the lander and surface habitat behind.

The 10-month trip back to Earth will take you around the sun, with a close flyby of the planet Venus. You won't be able to see the surface of Venus through the CO_2 clouds surrounding it.

ROCKET SCIENCE

For space travel, rockets are the only way to go. Here's your guide to the propulsion systems that will carry you to Mars and back.

You'll be getting a push into space thanks to Isaac Newton's Third Law of Motion:

For every action there is an equal and opposite reaction. That is, if you push on something, it pushes back on you.

ROCKET TYPES

On your trip to Mars you'll be propelled by three different types of rockets: two types of chemical rockets, and an ion rocket.

Chemical rockets get thrust from combustion, or burning. It's really a chemical reaction that combines fuel with oxygen to produce heat and gas. As the fuel burns in the rocket's combustion chamber, the hot, rapidly expanding gases shoot out of the exhaust nozzle. The reaction to this action pushes the rocket in the opposite direction.

SOLID FUEL CHEMICAL ROCKET

Hot, expanding gases shoot out of the exhaust nozzle.

Earthbound thrusters, such as jet engines, get their oxygen from the air. There's no air in space, so your spacecraft has to carry both fuel and oxygen.

Solid fuel and oxidizer (oxygen-bearing chemical).

Hollow space along the middle forms the combustion chamber. Fuel burns from the inside out.

LIQUID FUEL CHEMICAL ROCKET

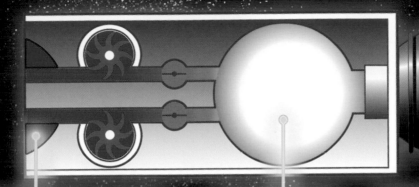

Tanks for liquid fuel (such as liquid hydrogen or methane) and oxidizer (such as liquid oxygen).

Fuel and oxidizer are pumped into the combustion chamber for burning.

Exhaust gases shoot out, propelling the rocket.

ION PROPULSION

Ion propulsion rockets get their power from ions (electrically charged atoms).

The tug's engine works by putting an electrical charge on atoms of fuel (xenon gas). These ions are then pushed out of the rocket by a pair of high-voltage electrical grids. The ions shoot out of the engine at 77,000 miles per hour, ten times faster than the gases in a chemical rocket.

KNOW YOUR ROCKET FUELS

Fuel Type	Solid	Liquid	Ion
Advantages	Starts faster—gives more acceleration at liftoff	More maximum thrust, which can be controlled	Can keep firing for a very long time (years instead of minutes)
Disadvantages	Thrust can't be shut off or controlled	Requires complex pumps and plumbing	Very weak thrust; reaching high speed takes time

GRAVITY

It's the force that holds the universe together. It can also be a real headache for astronauts: You have to escape Earth's gravity to get to Mars and escape Mars's gravity to return to Earth.

MASS, DISTANCE, AND FORCE

Every object in the universe attracts every other object. That's gravity. The amount of gravitational force between any two objects depends on the masses of the objects and the distance between them. The bigger the masses or the smaller the distance between them, the stronger the force.

If you need extra hand- or footholds in the ship, it's easy to make them from loops of duct tape.

LET'S SAY YOU WEIGH 100 POUNDS ON EARTH.

EARTH: 100 LBS

BECAUSE THE MOON HAS SO MUCH LESS MASS THAN EARTH, YOU WOULD WEIGH LESS.

MOON: 16.6 LBS

MARS HAS MORE MASS THAN THE MOON, BUT MUCH LESS THAN EARTH.

MARS: 37.7 LBS

JUPITER HAS FAR MORE MASS THAN ANY OTHER PLANET IN THE SOLAR SYSTEM.

JUPITER: 236.4 LBS

MAKING YOUR ESCAPE

To escape the pull of a planet's gravity, a spacecraft must accelerate to the speed called escape velocity. Escape velocity for Earth is 25,032 mph. That's right—when you are pushed out of Earth orbit, you'll be traveling faster than 25,000 miles per hour!

WEIGHTLESS DOESN'T MEAN GRAVITY-LESS

When you're weightless in orbit, it's not because you've escaped the planet's gravity. If you had, you wouldn't be in orbit. An orbit is like a fall that never ends.

Since the spacecraft and everyone and everything in it are all falling together, you don't feel the force of gravity.

SPACECRAFT'S MOMENTUM—ITS FORCE OF MOVEMENT—WOULD CARRY IT IN A STRAIGHT LINE.

IT "FALLS" BUT DOESN'T LOSE ANY ALTITUDE.

BUT THE FORCE OF GRAVITY PULLS IT DOWNWARD, CURVING ITS PATH.

AEROBRAKING: SLOW DOWN FOR MARS

Once your ship reaches Mars, it has to slow down enough to be held in orbit by the planet's gravity. Your ship will use aerobraking, dipping down into the planet's upper atmosphere to let friction reduce its speed. As the ship hits molecules in the atmosphere , those tiny collisions will slow it down. With careful navigation by the on-board computers, the craft will slow down and place itself in orbit around the Red Planet, ready for the next stage of your journey.

Your ship's heat-shielding aeroshell will keep you from becoming a flaming meteor.

LIFE SUPPORT

The ship's life support system supplies you with air, water, and food, takes away waste, and maintains temperature and pressure to keep you alive and well in the vacuum of space.

WASTE CONVERSION

The life support system processes waste from astronauts and creates water, oxygen, and waste that can be stored or vented from the ship.

LIFE SUPPORT SYSTEMS

INPUT FROM ASTRONAUTS

- CO_2
- EXHALED WATER VAPOR
- WASTE WATER
- URINE
- SOLID WASTE

OUTPUT FROM LIFE SUPPORT SYSTEMS

- METHANE (VENTED FROM SHIP)
- O_2
- WATER
- SLUDGE

BACKUP BACKUP BACKUP

Every system that is critical for your mission has a backup. Every system that the crew needs to stay alive has two backups. That's because if a machine or system fails, there won't be any rescue ship. You're on your own.

Sludge (called "brine") is left behind after urine and solid waste are boiled, and is then stored for disposal.

ABOUT THE AIR

The air in the Mars Transit Habitat is a lot like Earth's—20% oxygen and 80% nitrogen.

ZERO-GRAVITY TOILET

The space toilet works by air (suction) rather than water. Because there's no gravity to pull the wastes down, there has to be suction. (It's the cabin pressure!) There's also no gravity to hold you down on the seat. Instead, the thigh bar restraint holds you in place. Liquid content of the waste is transferred to the life support system.

COMMODE
Airflow does all the work.

The commode opening is very small. Aim is important!

THIGH BAR
When seated on the commode, put the bar across your thighs to hold yourself in place on the seat. You don't want to go floating away while you're sitting here!

URINAL
The urinal is a lot like a vacuum cleaner hose with a funnel at the end. You can use the urinal standing up or sitting down.

FOOT RESTRAINTS
For extra security or using the urinal while standing.

Each crew member is issued a personal urinal funnel, with different shapes to fit men and women. Don't lose yours!

LIVING SPACE

Here, in the Mars transfer habitat, is where you'll be spending the greatest amount of time on the trip. On this journey, getting there and back takes far longer than your time on Mars. Don't worry—there will be plenty to do.

1 **VIEW PORT**

2 **FOOD STORAGE**

3 **CONVECTION OVEN**

4 **FOOD PREPARATION AREA (GALLEY)**

5 **ENVIRONMENTAL CONTROL AND LIFE SUPPORT SYSTEMS (ECLSS)** supply oxygen and water, recycled from material supplied by the ship's air intake vents, toilet, shower, and waste system

6 **TOILET**

7 **MAIN COMMUNICATION ANTENNA**

The ECLSS, pronounced EE-kliss, can recover and purify about 93% of the water in the air and astronaut-supplied urine.

7

TIGHT QUARTERS

The habitat measures 27 feet across, and the same distance from end to end. But it's chock full of supplies and equipment, leaving a living space the size of a very small apartment for your four-member crew. On the other hand, there's a lot more room than there would be on Earth: without gravity there's no floor or ceiling, no up or down. All the space is usable.

8 MAIN COMMUNICATIONS PANEL Flight instruments, controls, and monitors

9 STORAGE

10 BED

11 SPACE SUIT STORAGE/ SLEEPING BAGS

12 SHOWER

13 FIRST AID AND MEDICAL SUPPLIES

14 SOLAR ARRAY

15 HATCH AND AIRLOCK This vehicle is only boarded from space, never on the ground. You'll only be using this to enter and exit to other space vehicles or to go outside the ship in an emergency.

LIFE ON THE SHIP

It's not a four-star hotel, but you'll find the ship's accommodations just fine for a person with your spirit of adventure.

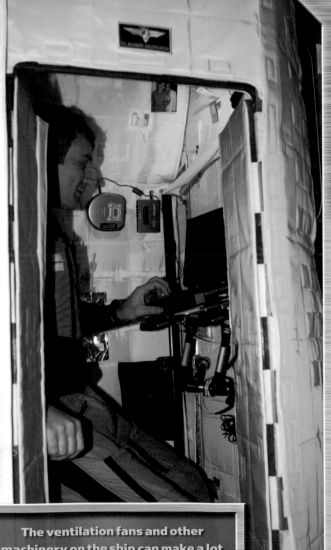

BEDROOM

In theory you could sleep anywhere you wanted on the ship, but you might be in for a rude awakening if you drifted into the wall or other object. You'll do best if you anchor your sleeping bag to the wall. Be sure to sleep near the air flow from a ventilator fan, or you'll wake up with a headache or worse from sleeping in your own exhaled carbon dioxide.

SHOWER

In space, a shower isn't the relaxing cascade of water you're used to. Surface tension makes water cling to objects, walls, and astronauts. If you're not careful, you can end up with water or other liquids stuck in your ears, eyes, or nose. You also don't want to get water on the ship's controls or machinery. Don't forget: There's no gravity to pull the water down the drain. That's why this one works by suction.

The ventilation fans and other machinery on the ship can make a lot of noise, so most astronauts choose to wear earplugs when they sleep.

The pros often prefer just to wash themselves with wet washcloths rather than using the shower. The water stays the cloth instead of floating around.

DINING

To save weight, much of the food is freeze-dried. You'll re-hydrate these meals with hot water from the life support system. You'll use the forced-air convection oven for heating meals. There's no microwave on the ship due to possible interference with the computers and communication system.

You'll find your sense of taste dulled in zero gravity. (Scientists aren't quite sure why.) Seasoned astronauts recommend space food with lots of herbs and spices.

RE-HYDRATABLE FOOD AND BEVERAGE CONTAINERS

You'll get to sample all of the food choices before leaving Earth. Then you can pick a personal menu plan with your favorite dishes.

A sample menu:

Breakfast: granola, Mexican scrambled eggs, coffee, orange juice

Lunch: peanut butter and jelly sandwich, dried apricots, chocolate pudding, lemonade

Dinner: mushroom soup, salmon, asparagus, potatoes au gratin, chocolate cookies, tea

Septum—water is injected into your food pouch using a large needle inserted through the end of this tube-like extension.

Drink container—stick a straw through the hole left by the needle, and sip away!

19

STAYING HEALTHY

You'll be millions of miles from the nearest hospital or doctor's office. Luckily, at least one member of every Mars crew has medical training.

HEALTHY AS AN ASTRONAUT

You're not likely to catch a cold or the flu on the trip. All astronauts spend time in quarantine, with no outside contact, before lifting off from Earth. That's to minimize the chance of anyone carrying germs aboard.

MEDICAL SUPPLIES

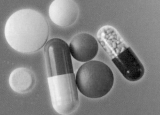

Medicines for treatment of pain, infection, nausea, and other problems.

Syringes and needles for intravenous injections.

First aid supplies, including sutures and needles for stitches.

Defibrillator, for delivering an electric shock to re-start the heart.

EMESIS (BARF) BAG

Make sure to keep one of these handy when you first get to space. Nearly half of all astronauts suffer from space sickness. Scientists still haven't completely figured out the biology, but they know the result: nausea and vomiting. Hang in there. Most people get over the sickness after the first few days of a mission.

Barf carefully. In zero-g, the vomit can bounce off the bottom of the bag and come back in your face.

DON'T FORGET TO BRUSH YOUR TEETH

You'll brush and floss your teeth just as you do on Earth. You can even take your own favorite toothpaste in your personal hygiene kit. But you won't be able to spit in the sink, because there isn't one. Instead, you'll have to spit the toothpaste into a tissue and throw it in the trash.

USE THEM OR LOSE THEM

With no gravity to resist them, your muscles and bones do only a fraction of the work in space that they have to do on Earth. Even your heart has less work to do. Without exercise, your cardiovascular system will weaken, your muscles will waste away, and your bones will grow weak and fragile. That's why it's important to keep up an exercise routine on the ship's gym equipment.

Zero-g causes all kinds of changes in your body. For one thing, you'll get taller in space—as much as 2 inches—because your spine will lengthen.

TREADMILL
Since there's no gravity, you'll have to strap yourself on with the bungee cord harness.

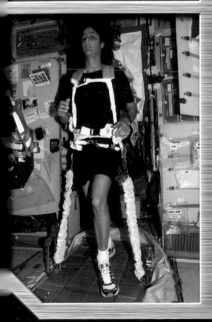

STATIONARY BICYCLE
No seat. You ride the bike standing up.

RESISTANCE EXERCISER
An arrangement of cords and wheels gives you a simulated weightlifting workout.

SPACE SUIT

The extravehicular space suit is your best friend for the all-important space walk. Everything you need—from food and water to oxygen and electricity—is within your suit. Get to know it well. With practice, you should be able to get everything on in 15 minutes.

> Extravehicular means "outside the vehicle." You wear this suit for taking trips outside the ship, but not for exploring the Martian surface.

1 VISOR ASSEMBLY
Includes an inner, gold-covered sun-filtering visor and an outer impact-protection visor, goes over the helmet. Don't forget the anti-fog compounds for the inside of your helmet.

2 COOLING AND VENTILATION GARMENT
Water circulates through tubes in the cloth to carry heat away from your body.

3 HARD UPPER TORSO (HUT)
Hard fiberglass shell, other parts of the suit attach here.

4 IN-SUIT DRINK BAG (IDB)
Attaches to inside of the upper torso assembly, flexible straw extends into the helmet.

5 MAXIMUM ABSORPTION GARMENT (MAG)
An adult-sized space diaper. (There are no bathroom breaks on a spacewalk!)

6 EXTRAVEHICULAR ACTIVITY (EVA) GLOVE
The EVA gloves go on last for a reason. Fine motor control is greatly reduced when you're wearing them!

> Astronauts love abbreviations and acronyms. Never say "maximum absorption garment" when you can say MAG. Likewise, EVA, HUT, etc. POC (piece of cake)!

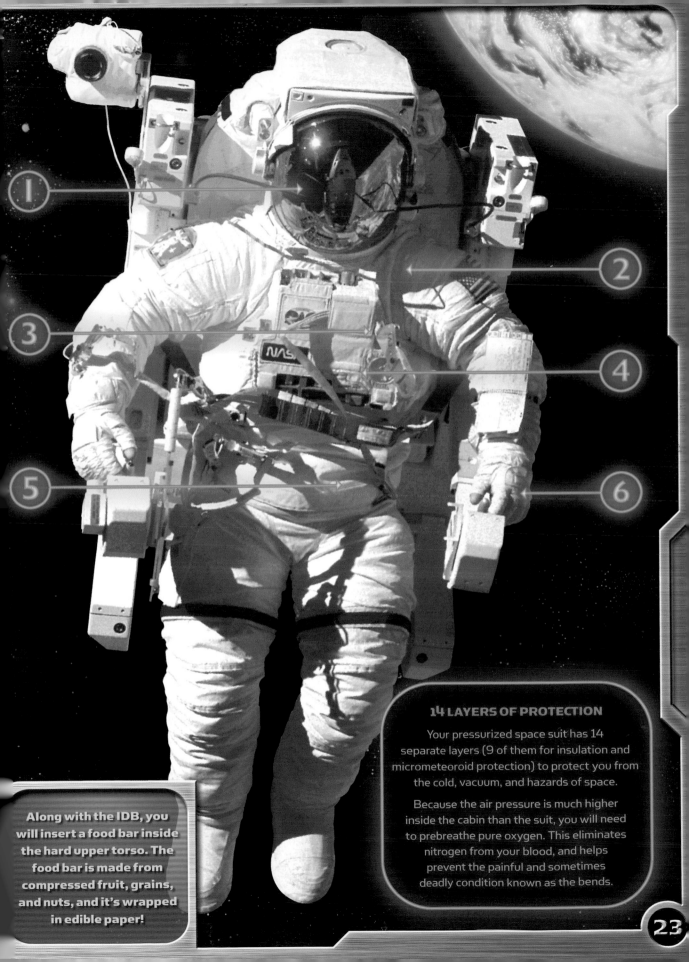

1

2

3

4

5

6

14 LAYERS OF PROTECTION

Your pressurized space suit has 14 separate layers (9 of them for insulation and micrometeoroid protection) to protect you from the cold, vacuum, and hazards of space.

Because the air pressure is much higher inside the cabin than the suit, you will need to prebreathe pure oxygen. This eliminates nitrogen from your blood, and helps prevent the painful and sometimes deadly condition known as the bends.

Along with the IDB, you will insert a food bar inside the hard upper torso. The food bar is made from compressed fruit, grains, and nuts, and it's wrapped in edible paper!

POWER AND COM SYSTEMS

Your spacecraft's computer systems are the brains of the ship. The communication system lets you keep in touch with Mission Control and the folks back home. The ship's power plant provides the electricity that keeps everything on board running.

SOLAR ARRAY

When you're in orbit or coasting between planets, your main power source is the sun. With the ship's long array of solar panels extended and aimed at the sun, the solar power system produces more than 30 kilowatts of electricity, enough to run all of the ships systems.

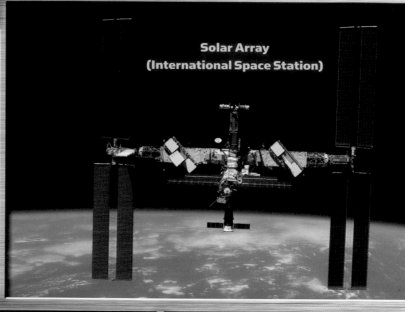

**Solar Array
(International Space Station)**

FUEL CELLS

In addition to solar energy, your ship gets electricity from fuel cells. These produce electricity by combining hydrogen and oxygen. The "waste" product from fuel cells is pure water for the crew and the oxygen-producing life-support system.

Like everything else aboard, your ship's electrical power has three levels of redundancy. In other words, there's a power plant, backup power, and backup backup power.

Fuel Cell Diagram

HYDROGEN
ANODE
ELECTROLYTE
CATHODE
OXYGEN

H H H H H H H H H H H
O O O O O O O
H O H O H O H

CATALYST   CATALYST

EXCESS HYDROGEN (FOR REUSE) H_2 ELECTRIC POWER H_2O WATER

COMMUNICATION

All of your communication with Earth, whether it's audio, video, or computer data, is carried by radio waves. Even though radio waves travel at the speed of light, 186,000 miles per second, you're going the farthest that humans have ever traveled. Depending on the positions of the planets, it can take longer than 20 minutes for a radio transmission to travel between Mars and Earth. Even at the closest distance it's still more than three minutes between the time you say "Hello" and someone on Earth can hear it.

COMPUTERS

The ship's computers handle life support, flight control, navigation, and communication with Earth. They also contain information on all of the equipment and tasks of your mission. There's even an e-mail program for sending messages back to Earth.

WIRELESS

A lightweight headset and transmitter let you use the audio communication system while moving freely around the ship. The transmitter sends and receives signals from a wall unit, which is connected to the ship's audio communication system.

YOU'RE A STAR

Video cameras on the ship let mission control see what happens on board. They'll always ask permission before turning on the cameras, and you can always turn them off for privacy.

The radio link carrying communication from Earth to you is called the uplink. The connection from you back to Earth is called the downlink.

SURFACE MISSION

There's not much time for sightseeing. You'll have lots to do, and only a month to do it.

POWER SYSTEM—
cells and solar po...

ASCENT MODULE—
for return trip to Earth

LIVING OFF THE LAND

To see if it's possible to live off the raw materials of the Martian atmosphere, you'll be trying out a machine to make oxygen and fuel out of thin air. Or what passes for air on Mars— in other words, carbon dioxide (CO_2). This gas makes up 95% of the Martian atmosphere. (It's not even 1% of Earth's atmosphere.)

Much like the ECLSS on your ship, the Martian machine takes in hydrogen (which you'll bring with you) and CO_2, and puts out oxygen and methane. Instead of being thrown away, the methane will be saved in liquid form to be used as fuel. That means future Martian colonists will be able to make their own fuel for both fuel cells and spacecraft. That leaves more weight available on ships from Earth for supplies and equipment.

NASA

ROVER—all-wheel drive gives you traction in the sandy soil

Take it slow and easy. After seven months of weightlessness, it will take you a while to adjust to even the low gravity of Mars.

MARTIAN JOBS

Here are a few of the jobs you'll perform on the surface mission:

CONSTRUCTION WORKER

You'll be putting up components to test them for an eventual permanent Mars base, including the Mars surface habitat you arrived in as well as a small inflatable greenhouse.

PROSPECTOR

You'll be looking for evidence of underground water or other resources that can be used to support a future Mars base.

BIOLOGIST

You'll be looking for signs of life, past or present.

EXPLORER

You'll be making excursions by foot and rover, seeing sights no human has ever witnessed before.

FARMER

You'll be tending plants and trying out techniques that will eventually supply Martian colonists with food and oxygen. You're carrying the seeds with you, but there's no room to grow them in the transit habitat. On Mars, not only will the plants take carbon dioxide out of the air and put out oxygen, they'll also provide you with tasty fresh food.

SURFACE HABITAT

AIRLOCK

REMOTE CONTROL ROCKET

You don't have to be a rocket scientist to launch this rocket, but it does take some preparation. You'll have more fun if you read all the instructions before you try to launch your rocket.

YOUR KIT INCLUDES:
Rocket cylinder, cap, launch pad, and remote control

YOU'LL NEED:
White vinegar, baking soda/bicarbonate of soda, plastic bowl, meauring cup, and paper towels

What Americans call "baking soda" is called "bicarbonate of soda" in the UK and ROI. What is called "baking soda" in the UK and ROI is what Americans call "baking powder," which will not work to power the rocket.

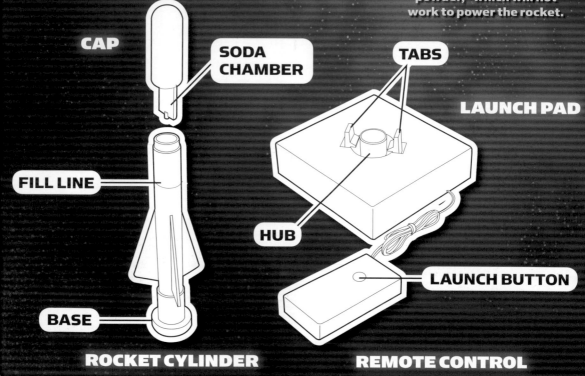

CAP

SODA CHAMBER

TABS

LAUNCH PAD

FILL LINE

HUB

BASE

ROCKET CYLINDER

LAUNCH BUTTON

REMOTE CONTROL

A few very important things to remember about your rocket:

- **WARNING: DO NOT STAND OVER A LOADED ROCKET! AFTER LOADING THE BAKING SODA/BICARBONATE OF SODA, STEP BACK FOUR FEET—AS FAR AS THE REMOTE CONTROL WILL ALLOW.**
- **Adult supervision is required.**
- **This is an outdoor toy—never play with it inside the house.**
- **Never point your rocket at anyone.**
- **Do not move the rocket once you have started the launch process.**
- **Do not try to catch the rocket as it flies through the air! Pick it up after it lands.**

1) INSTALL THE BATTERIES IN THE REMOTE CONTROL

Use a screwdriver to remove the cover of the battery compartment on the underside of the remote control. Insert two 1.5v AAA batteries, making sure they're facing the right direction, as shown in the battery illustration. Screw the cover back on.

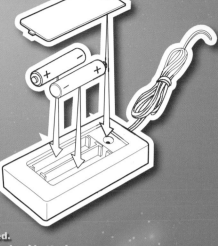

Battery Cautions:
- Insert batteries with the correct polarity.
- Do not short-circuit the supply terminals.
- Remove exhausted batteries from the toy.
- Do not recharge nonrechargeable batteries.
- Batteries are small objects and could be ingested.
- Never let a child use this product unless the battery door is secure.
- Remove rechargeable batteries from the toy before charging them.
- Only use batteries of the same or equivalent type as recommended.
- Rechargeable batteries are only to be charged under adult supervision.
- Different types of batteries or new and used batteries are not to be mixed.
- Do not mix alkaline, standard (carbon-zinc), or rechargeable (nickel-cadmium) batteries.
- Keep all batteries away from small children, and immediately dispose of any batteries safely.
- To ensure proper safety and operation, battery replacement must always be done by an adult.

2) GATHER YOUR SUPPLIES

Your rocket is fueled by vinegar and baking soda/bicarbonate of soda. Ask an adult to help you find some plain white vinegar and a box of baking soda/bicarbonate of soda. Get a small plastic bowl and dump in about ½ cup of baking soda/bicarbonate of soda.

3) TEST THE EQUIPMENT

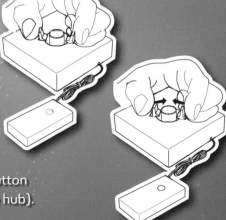

Tabs in locked position (not up against hub)

Wiggle the tabs on the launch pad. If you can easily move the tabs all the way against the hub, they're in the unlocked position. If the tabs are difficult to squeeze together, they're in the locked position. The tabs need to be in the unlocked position for you to attach the rocket cylinder to the launch pad.

To unlock the tabs, press the launch button on the remote control and hold it down while gently squeezing the tabs together. You will hear the motor running inside the launch pad. Stop pressing the launch button when the tabs are in the unlocked position (up against the hub). Now the tabs should be unlocked.

If the tabs are in the locked position, don't force them open or closed! Continue to hold down the launch button until they unlock.

Tabs in unlocked position (up against hub)

4) ATTACH YOUR ROCKET TO THE LAUNCH PAD

Unscrew the cap from the nose of the rocket and set it aside. Set the tabs on the launch pad to the unlocked position. Set the rocket cylinder in the hole on the launch pad. Squeeze the tabs together until they click into the locked position covering the base of the rocket. This secures the rocket in place.

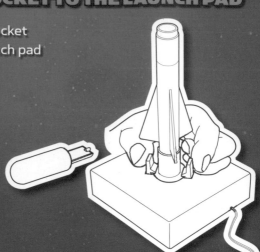

5) LOAD THE FUEL

Fill the rocket cylinder with vinegar up to the fill line (about 4 teaspoons). Pour out any excess vinegar. If there is too much vinegar in the cylinder, it will leak out during launch.

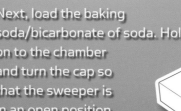

FILL LINE

**Sweeper closed—
twist to open**

Next, load the baking soda/bicarbonate of soda. Hold on to the chamber and turn the cap so that the sweeper is in an open position.

Sweeper open

Dip the soda chamber into the bowl of baking soda/bicarbonate of soda and scoop out a good amount. Then, turn the cap so that the sweeper closes over the chamber. As you do this, excess baking soda/bicarbonate of soda will spill out. Don't worry—the chamber is designed to hold the right amount of baking soda/bicarbonate of soda (about 1/2 teaspoon). Use your hand to brush any excess baking soda/bicarbonate of soda off of the outside of the chamber.

6) COUNT DOWN TO BLAST-OFF

When you are ready to launch your rocket, you need to work quickly. Screw the cap onto the rocket as tightly as possible. The reaction begins as soon as the baking soda/bicarbonate of soda is loaded.

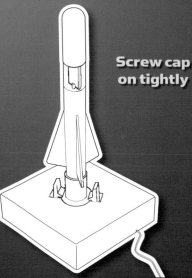

Screw cap on tightly

Step back as far as the remote cord will allow. (Do not pull on the launch pad with the remote cord.) Count down four seconds, then press the launch button, (for about seven seconds) until the tabs release and the rocket blasts off.

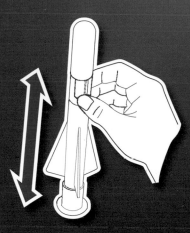

Experiment with how many seconds you count down before pressing the launch button. How high does the rocket fly after waiting five or six seconds?

You can also try giving the rocket a shake immediately after screwing on the cap to mix the fuel. Keep the rocket pointed straight up and down. Gently shake the rocket up and down one or two times. Then set the rocket down and proceed with your launch.

Be safe! If the rocket misfires—for instance, if only one tab releases—wait for the fizzing reaction to stop. If you see that fuel is leaking from the base of the rocket, do not try to fix it. If the rocket starts to come unattached from the launch pad, do not investigate. If either of these things happens, stand back, and push the launch button to release the rocket. Then ask an adult to remove the rocket from the launch pad.

ROCKET MAINTENANCE

Every launch works better with clean, dry equipment.

Wipe off the launch pad with a damp paper towel and then a dry paper towel. Do not immerse or rinse the launch pad in water or any other liquid!

Rinse the rocket cylinder and cap with water. Clean out any leftover baking soda/bicarbonate of soda. Use a paper towel to get the soda chamber as dry as possible.

When you're done launching and experimenting, let the launch pad and rocket parts air-dry completely before you put them away.

The tabs on the launch pad may be in the locked position after a launch. It is necessary to unlock the tabs before you can set up the rocket for another launch. See step 3 to review.

STICKER INSTRUCTIONS

Make sure the rocket is clean and dry before you apply the stickers.

Apply these stickers to both sides of the fins.

Wrap this sticker around the rocket just above the base.

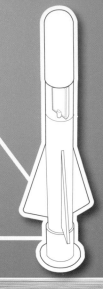

TROUBLESHOOTING

- **Rocket not launching high enough?** Experiment with the amount of vinegar in the fuel mixture. If you use slightly less vinegar and wait a few more seconds before you press the launch button, you may get a bigger blast-off. Also, your baking soda/bicarbonate of soda could be old. New baking soda/bicarbonate of soda works better than old baking soda/bicarbonate of soda.

- **Fuel leaking from the bottom of the rocket?** This means that the rocket was not properly attached to the launch pad. Check the tabs on the launch pad before your next launch. Make sure the tabs are locked to the base of the rocket.

- **Vinegar fizzing when poured into cylinder?** The cylinder still had some baking soda/bicarbonate of soda in it. Wash and dry the cylinder thoroughly between launches.

- **Baking soda/bicarbonate of soda fizzing out the top when added to cylinder?** You could have too much vinegar in the cylinder. Wash and dry the cylinder thorough and start again.

- **Baking soda/bicarbonate of soda clumping inside chamber?** The soda chamber was not thoroughly dry.

- **Fuel overflowing during launch?** You used too much vinegar or baking soda/bicarbonate of soda (or both). The cap was not screwed on correctly. (Or it wasn't screwed on tightly enough.)